More titles from Finding My Way Books
Otros títulos de Finding My Way Books

I Want To Be Like Poppin' Joe
Yo quiero ser como Joe Palomitas
Kaitlyn Wants To See Ducks
Kaitlyn quiere ver patos
I Don't Know If I Want a Puppy
Yo no sé si quiero un perrito
Marco and I Want To Play Ball
Marco y yo queremos jugar al béisbol
OE Wants It To Be Friday
OE quiere que sea viernes

Early Reader Chapter Book

Reese Has a Halloween Secret
Reese tiene un secreto de Halloween

Growing With Grace Series

MyaGrace Wants To Make Music
MyaGrace quiere hacer música (Spanish only)
MyaGrace Wants To Make Music/MyaGrace quiere hacer música
MyaGrace Wants To Get Ready
MyaGrace Wants To Get Ready/MyaGrace quiere alistarse

Finding My World Series

Neema Wants To Learn

MyaGrace Wants To Get Ready

A True Story Promoting Inclusion and Self-Determination

Growing With Grace Series
Book Two

MyaGrace quiere alistarse

Una historia que promueve la inclusión y la autodeterminación
Serie Creciendo con gracia
Libro Dos

By/De Jo Meserve Mach
Vera Lynne Stroup-Rentier

Photography by/Fotografías de Mary Birdsell

Translation by/Traducción de
Karen Anchante

TOPEKA, KANSAS

Library of Congress Control Number: 2016913964

Paperback ISBN: 978-1-9447640-1-2
Hardcover ISBN: 978-1-9447640-2-9

Spanish translation by Karen Anchante

Finding My Way Books
honoring children with special needs or
disabilities by sharing their stories
www.findingmywaybooks.com

Finding My Way Books is dedicated to celebrating the success
of inclusion by sharing stories about children with
special needs in families and communities.

Finding My Way Books se dedica a celebrar el éxito de la inclusión
al compartir historias acerca de niños con necesidades
especiales en las familias y las comunidades.

We celebrate MyaGrace's story!

MyaGrace was adopted from India to the US when she was two years old. She was very small for her age and had difficulty eating. MyaGrace has Cerebral Palsy, Autism and intellectual disabilities. Today she is an enthusiastic teenager wanting to experience life as fully as possible.

We chose to write this story because it demonstrates how teenage girls with disabilities want to be included in activities with their friends and classmates, just like every teenager out there. With support that is encouraging and respectful, MyaGrace shows us how she is learning skills needed for her self-determination.

We wish to share with you the pure joy that is revealed in this story,
~Jo, Vera and Mary

Por qué festejamos la historia de MyaGrace.

MyaGrace fue adoptada de la India y llegó a los EE.UU. cuando tenía dos años. Ella era muy pequeña para su edad y tenía dificultades para comer. MyaGrace tiene parálisis cerebral, autismo y discapacidad intelectual. Hoy ella es una adolescente entusiasta con ganas de experimentar la vida plenamente.

Nosotras elegimos escribir esta historia porque muestra cómo las niñas adolescentes con discapacidades quieren ser incluidas en actividades con sus amigos y compañeros de clase, al igual que todos los demás adolescentes. Con el apoyo de una familia que la alienta y la respeta, MyaGrace nos muestra cómo ella está aprendiendo habilidades necesarias para su autodeterminación.

Deseamos compartir con ustedes la felicidad plena que se revela en esta historia.
~Jo, Vera and Mary

Hi, my name is MyaGrace.
I play piano.

Hola, mi nombre ese MyaGrace.
Yo toco piano.

1

My family and I like music.
We listen to music all the time.

A mi familia y a mí nos gusta la música.
Escuchamos música todo el tiempo.

I like dance music the best. I love to dance.
My brother, Ethan, likes to dance with me.

Me gusta más la música bailable. Me encanta bailar.
A mi hermano Ethan le gusta bailar conmigo.

My friend, Emily, sent me a message. There's going to be a dance. I want to go. I'll ask Mom.

Mi amiga Emily me ha enviado un mensaje. Va a haber un baile. Quiero ir. Le pediré permiso a mamá.

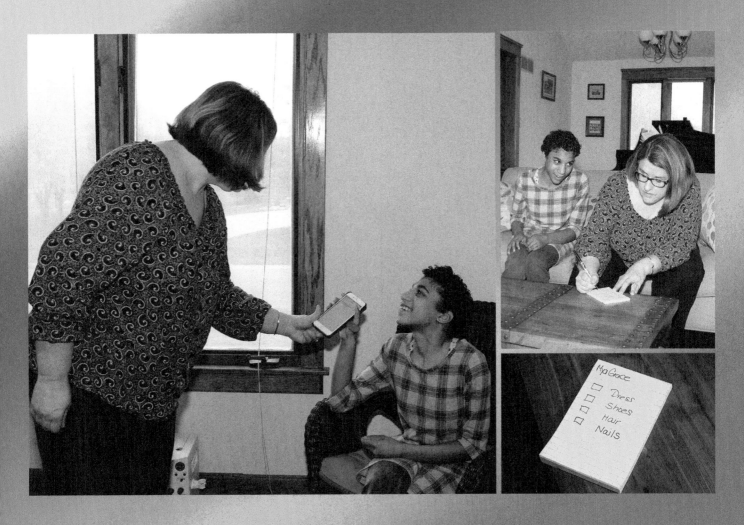

Mom says I can go. Hooray!
Now I need to get ready. Mom helps me make a list.

Mamá dice que puedo ir. ¡Hurra!
Ahora necesito alistarme. Mamá me ayuda a hacer una lista.

"MyaGrace, I borrowed some dresses.
Are you ready to try them on?" "Just a minute, I'll get ready."

"MyaGrace, me prestaron algunos vestidos.
¿Estás lista para probártelos?"
"Estaré lista en un minuto".

6

I show Mom the dress I like. She says it's too big.
That's okay. I'll pick another dress.

Le muestro a mamá el vestido que me gusta.
Ella dice que es demasiado grande.
Esta bien. Voy a escoger otro vestido.

I'll be cold in this one.
I can't walk in this one.

Tendré frío con éste.
No puedo caminar en éste.

I like this color. It's purple and it shines.
I can't wait to tell Emily about my dress.

Me gusta este color. Es morado y brilla.
Tengo muchas ganas de contarle a Emily sobre mi vestido.

I want to practice dancing in my dress.
"Ethan, come dance."

Quiero practicar bailar con mi vestido puesto.
"Ethan, ven a bailar".

What else do I need to get ready?
I check my list.

¿Qué más necesito para alistarme?
Reviso mi lista.

"MyaGrace, I have some new shoes.
Are you ready to try them on?" "Just a minute, I'll get ready."

"MyaGrace, tengo unos zapatos nuevos para tí.
¿Estás lista para probártelos?"
"Estaré lista en un minuto".

12

I show Mom the boots I like. She says they aren't dress shoes.
I need to pick different shoes.

Le muestro a mamá las botas que me gustan.
Ella dice que no son zapatos de vestir.
Tengo que escoger otros zapatos.

These shoes are pretty.
The color goes with my dress.

Estos zapatos son bonitos.
El color va con mi vestido.

Can I dance in these shoes? I need to practice.
"Ethan, will you dance with me again?"

¿Podré bailar con estos zapatos? Necesito practicar.
"Ethan, ¿puedes bailar conmigo otra vez?"

15

I like these shoes. I can dance in them.
I need to show Emily. Mom is trying to take a picture.

Me gustan estos zapatos. Puedo bailar con ellos.
Necesito mostrarle a Emily.
Mamá está tratando de tomar una foto.

I pick out what else I want to wear.
This will help me get ready.

Escojo qué más quiero ponerme.
Esto me ayudará a alistarme.

Now I know what comes next.
Hair and nails are what I like best.

Ahora sé lo que viene a continuación.
Hacerme un peinado y arreglarme las uñas es lo
que más me gusta.

The dance is tonight.
Lori is going to help me get ready.

El baile es esta noche.
Lori me va a ayudar a alistarme.

19

I love coming to Lori's shop. I like to help Lori.
Mom gets her hair done first.

Me encanta venir al salón de belleza de Lori.
Me gusta ayudar a Lori.
Mamá es la primera en hacerse el peinado.

Now I need to pick my nail color.
There are so many colors. I found it!

Ahora tengo que elegir el color que quiero para mis uñas.
Hay tantos colores. ¡Lo encontré!

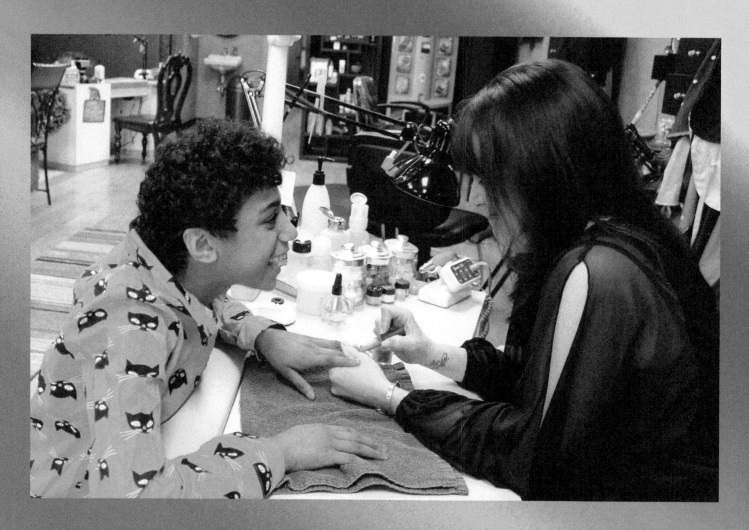

"It looks good.
Thank you, Lori."

"Se ve bien.
Gracias, Lori ".

22

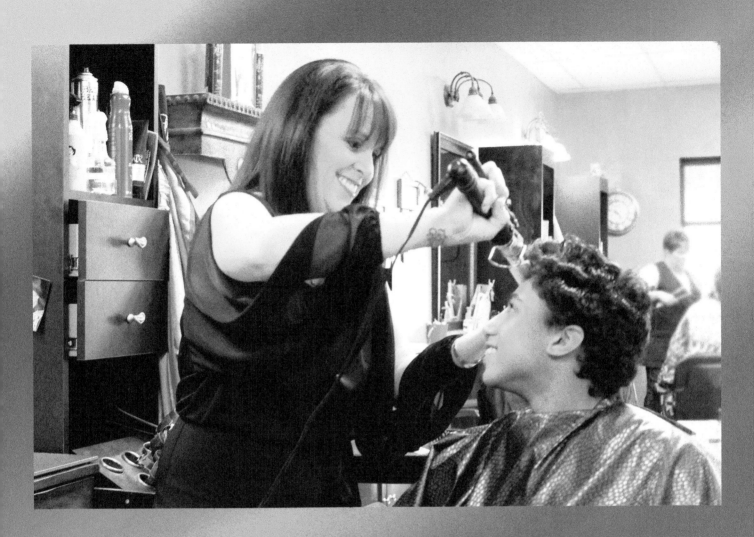

It's time to do my hair.

Es hora de hacer mi peinado.

"How does it look?"
Lori says my hair looks good. I like it!

"¿Cómo se ve?"
Lori dice que mi cabello se ve bien. ¡Me gusta!

Mom and Lori have a surprise for me.
I'm getting makeup.

Mamá y Lori tienen una sorpresa para mí.
Me estoy poniendo maquillaje.

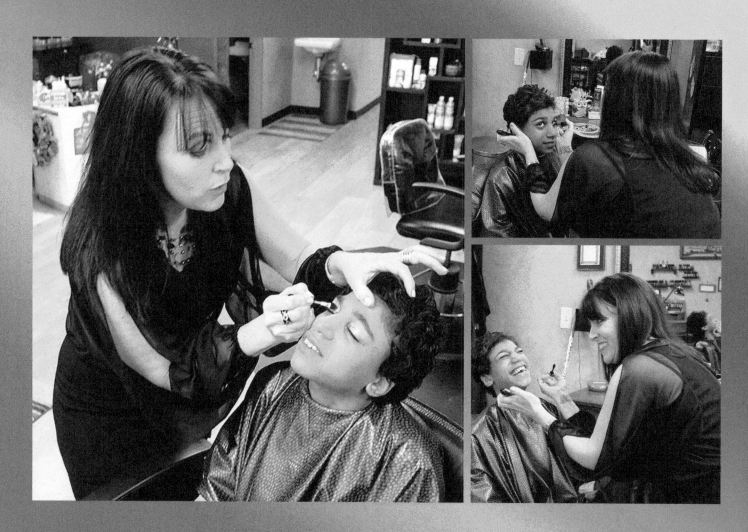

"Are we done yet?"
Lori says we're not done yet. "I love it already!"

"¿Ya terminamos?"
Lori dice que no hemos terminado todavía.
"¡Pero ya me encanta!"

I love makeup. I want my lipstick just like Lori's.
"Thank you, Lori, for doing my makeup." What a great surprise.

Amo el maquillaje.
Quiero que mi lapiz de labios se vea como el de Lori.
"Gracias Lori, por maquillarme." Qué gran sorpresa.

I look great!

¡Me veo muy bien!

My list is done.
I've got to go home and get ready.

Hice todo lo de mi lista.
Tengo que ir a casa y alistarme.

Emily is coming over soon.
I'm ready to dance!

Emily va a venir.
¡Estoy lista para bailar!

Mom is good at helping.
I'm almost ready.

Mamá es buena ayudando.
Estoy casi lista.

I want to finish by myself.
Now I'm ready.

Quiero terminar de alistarme yo sola.
Ahora estoy lista.

"MyaGrace, Emily's here.
Are you ready?"

"MyaGrace, Emily ya llegó.
¿Estás lista?"

We're ready!

¡Estamos listas!

34

Thank you to MyaGrace, her family and friends for sharing their story.

MyaGrace wants you to know she danced every dance
and had a wonderful time at her school dance.

Gracias a MyaGrace, a su familia y a sus amigos por
compartir su historia.

MyaGrace quiere que sepas que ella bailó todas las canciones
y la pasó maravillosamente en su baile de la escuela.

RESOURCES

Pg. 39 Information about self-determination

Pgs. 40-45 *Discussion Starters* and *Activities* to promote self-determination

Pg. 47 Information about Finding My Way Books

Pg. 49 Contact information

Encouraging self-determination skill building in children

Our books are written in the actual voice of a child. The child is telling their story of how they are learning to be more self-determined.

Here are examples of self-determination skills:
1. Choice making
2. Decision making
3. Problem solving
4. Goal setting and planning
5. Self-direction behaviors (self-regulation)
6. Responsibility
7. Independence
8. Self-awareness and self-knowledge
9. Self-advocacy and leadership
10. Communication
11. Participation
12. Having relationships and social connections

Weir, K., Cooney, M., Walter, M., Moss, C., & Carter, E. W. (2011). Fostering self-determination among children with disabilities: Ideas from parents for parents. *Madison, WI: Natural Supports Project, Waisman Center, University of Wisconsin—Madison.*

Discussion Starters and Activities To Promote Self-Determination

For Building on Interests and Self Awareness
Story pages building on interests: 5, 7, 10, 12, 16, 19-28
Story pages demonstrating self-awareness: 16, 22, 24, 26, 28

Discussion Starter:
Going to a school dance is one of MyaGrace's favorite things to do. It includes everything she loves. She loves music and dancing. She loves getting her hair, nails and makeup done. MyaGrace knows what she likes and she knows she looks good. What is your favorite activity? Is it a time when you are more aware of how you feel?

Classroom activity:
Have your students write their name and favorite activity on a piece of paper. Collect all the papers and collate the activities to create lists of students with shared interests.

Divide the class by their shared interests. Ask each group to put their ideas together and create a super fun activity. Have each group share their activity with the class. Ask students to share how they feel when they're getting to do their favorite activity.

For Choice Making
Story pages demonstrating choice making: 14, 17, 21

Discussion Starter:
MyaGrace makes several choices as she gets ready to go to the dance.
Can you remember the choices she made? Why did she make those choices?

Classroom activity:
Have each student write a description or draw a picture of a choice they
made today. Ask students to share why they made that choice.

For Decision Making
Story pages demonstrating decision-making: 8, 9

Discussion Starter:
MyaGrace had to make a decision about what to wear. She didn't just
choose the dress she liked. She took time to think about each dress and
determine which one would be best for her to wear to the dance. What are
the things she thought about as she made her decision?

Classroom Acitivity:
Dances often have have themes. Have students think of a theme for a school
dance. List the ideas on the board. Review the list and ask students to share
what they like or don't like about each idea. Have the class vote to select the
best theme. Discuss their decision making process.

For Problem Solving

Story pages demonstrating problem solving: 10, 13, 15

Discussion Starter:
MyaGrace's problem was she loved to wear her boots. Her mother told her that her boots didn't go with her dress. She had to choose other shoes to wear and she had to be sure they would be good for dancing. How did she figure out if the shoes she chose would be good dancing shoes? Talk about a time someone told you that you weren't wearing the right thing for an occasion. What did you do to solve your problem?

Classroom activity:
Divide the class into a group of girls and a group of boys. Set up a competition to see which group can more quickly solve the problems on this list: (Each problem is solved by changing what they are wearing.)

1. The windows won't close and it's really windy!
2. The water pipes are broken and our room is flooded!
3. Our school turned into a swimming pool!
4. There's a blizzard and it's time to get on the bus!
5. The workers on the roof are making the ceiling come down in pieces!
6. We forgot that it's Halloween!
7. It's dark outside and it's time to go to sleep.

For Participation and Relationships
Story pages demonstrating participation: 6-9, 13, 14, 17, 21
Story pages demonstrating relationships: 4, 9, 10, 15, 16, 19-28

Discussion Starter:
MyaGrace fully participated in all the activities that helped her get ready to go to the dance. Other people were also a part of the activities. She didn't do them all by herself. What are some of the activities she did with others? What have you done with your family or friends, when you've been part of the planning? How did that make you feel?

Classroom activity:
Have students sit quietly and listen to a song. Then have students move their desks and dance to a song.   Have students share how they felt listening (by themselves) compared to participating by dancing (interacting with others).

For Self-Direction and Independence

Story pages demonstrating self-direction and independence: 10, 13, 15, 19

Discussion Starter:
MyaGrace shows her mom the boots she could wear to the dance. She shares her dress and shoes with Lori. She helps Lori at the beauty shop. She practices dancing with her brother. What did you do today without being told what to do? How do you feel when you do things by yourself?

Classroom activity:
Divide the class into small groups of two to three students. Provide each group with one of the situations listed below. Ask them to think of one or two things they could do to make the situation better.

1. Three students at the school dance are sitting by themselves looking sad.
2. A student falls down while dancing.
3. All of a sudden the music stops at the dance.
4. Two students bump into each other and start fighting.
5. All the songs are in English and some of the students speak another language so they don't understand the words.
6. A student doesn't have anyone pick them up to take them home after the dance.

For Goal Setting

Story pages demonstrating goal setting: 5, 11, 18, 29

Discussion Starter:
MyaGrace's mother helped her make a list so she had goals to complete to be ready for her dance. How did MyaGrace keep track of what she had done on her list? Talk about a time you made a list. Who else do you know who makes lists? Why do they make lists?

Classroom activity:
Have each student make a list of five things they need to do to be ready to come to school. Have students share their lists with the student sitting beside them. Ask them to compare the tasks on their lists to look for similarities and differences.

Free downloadable lessons are available at: findingmywaybooks.com

Additional resources, linked to Finding My Way book titles, are available at:
teacherspayteachers.com

Jo Meserve Mach, author and publisher, spent 36 years as an Occupational Therapist. She is very passionate about sharing the stories of children with special needs. Jo embraces the joy that individuals with disabilities bring to our communities through their unique gifts.

Vera Lynne Stroup-Rentier, author, was an Early Childhood and Special Education teacher for 25 years. She has a PhD in Special Education from the University of Kansas and is currently working at the Kansas State Department of Education. Vera is passionate about the inclusion of each and every child in settings where they would be if they did not have a disability. Parenting a teen and tween with special needs enrich her life.

Mary Birdsell is a freelance photographer and a former Speech and Theatre teacher. She strives to create images that reflect the strengths of each child. Mary's background in education, theatre and photography intersect as she visually creates our books. She uses colors and shapes to tell a story. For her, each book is like it's own theatrical production.

Karen Anchante, translator, has over 20 years of experience teaching languages. She has a Ph.D. in Spanish from Arizona State University. As a mother of two young children, she loves contributing to enriching projects that benefit children. She is also a fervent believer of the effective power of reading from an early age.

For more information about all of our titles:
www.findingmywaybooks.com

Contact us:
info@findingmywaybook.com

CPSIA information can be obtained
at www.ICGtesting.com
Printed in the USA
LVOW06*1912100217
523875LV00022B/259/P